This edition published 2005 by
Mercury Books
20 Bloomsbury Street
London WC1B 3JH
ISBN 1-904668-75-5

Publisher: Felicia Law
Design director: Tracy Carrington
Project manager: Karen Foster
Author: Gerry Bailey
Editor: Rosalind Beckman
Designed by: Jacqueline Palmer
assisted by Simon Brewster, Will Webster
Cartoon illustrations: Steve Boulter (Advocate)
Make-and-do: Jan Smith
Model-maker: Tim Draper
Photo studio: Steve Lumb
Photo research: Diana Morris
Scanning: Imagewrite
Digital workflow: Edward MacDermott

Printed by D 2 Print Singapore

Photo Credits
AKG Images: 9t, 13t. Brooks & Brown/SPL: 21t.
Corbis: 42b. Tony Craddock/SPL: 6b.
Martin Dohrn/SPL: 29t. A.B.Dowsett/SPL: 18b.
Eye of Science/SPL: 10b.
Michael Greenlar/Image Works/Topham: 25t.
David Guyon, The BOC Group PLC/SPL: 14b.
Bob Mahoney/Image Works/Topham: 26b.
Larry Mulvehill/SPL: 41t.
Science Museum, London/HIP/Topham: 5t.
Prof. K. Seddon & Dr. T Evans, Queen's University, Belfast/SPL: 30b.
Silver Clef Productions Ltd/Rex Features: 38b. SPL: 17t, 33t, 37t.
Sean Sprague/Still Pictures: 22b. Geoff Tompkinson/SPL: 34b.

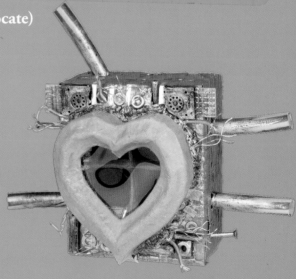

Crafty Inventions

MEDICAL MARVELS

Contents

Mercury Junior

20 BLOOMSBURY STREET
LONDON WC1B 3JH

How can I replace lost teeth?

People have always had problems with their teeth. Pre-historic people probably broke theirs by chewing on bones or in accidents. The ancient civilisations - the Egyptians, Greeks and Romans - all had remedies for toothache, including extraction.

In time, however, people in early civilisations learned to replace a few teeth, using bridges that connect a false tooth to a real one.

These bridges were usually made of gold, so only the rich could afford them. For most people who lost of their teeth, gums had to do!

Until the 1750s, barbers were also surgeons and dentists. But their methods were brutal, and dentistry was messy and painful. Many people's teeth were in a bad way. If only they could buy a new set.

Wouldn't it be great to replace broken and diseased teeth with a new, clean set?

WHAT DID THEY DO?

- Dental craftsmen tried to work out how to get a complete set of teeth to stay put in the mouth without falling out.

- In 1728 Pierre Fauchard, a French dentist, published *The Surgeon Dentist*. Someone was taking the problem seriously.

- Dentists realised that if false teeth are to fit, they need a base that makes contact with every single part of the gums and mouth.

- To do this, they would need to make a mould of the patient's mouth, using a material that hardened quickly - but did not stick to the gums.

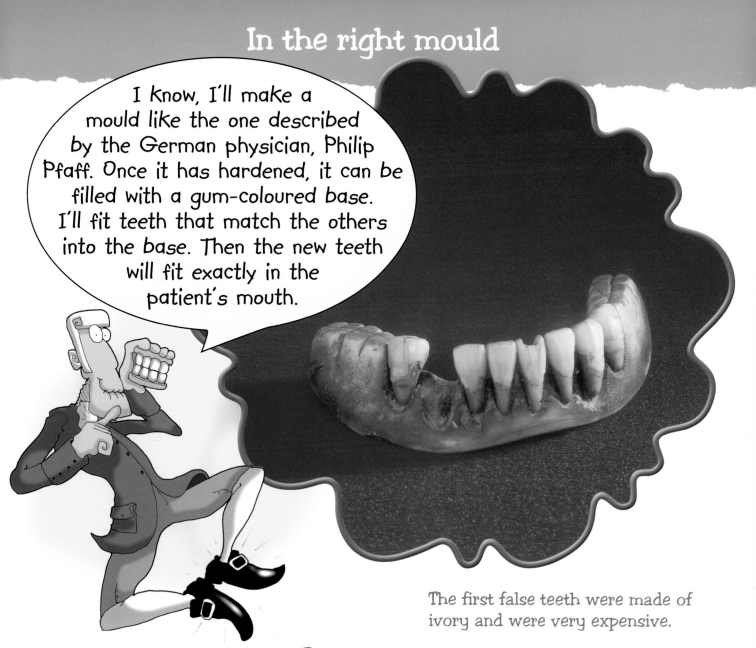

I know, I'll make a mould like the one described by the German physician, Philip Pfaff. Once it has hardened, it can be filled with a gum-coloured base. I'll fit teeth that match the others into the base. Then the new teeth will fit exactly in the patient's mouth.

The first false teeth were made of ivory and were very expensive.

A good impression

False teeth are artificial teeth that can be used in place of natural teeth. When artificial teeth are fitted, an **impression**, or likeness, is taken from the patient's mouth. This is made by pressing a plasticine-like substance, which hardens to make a mould, on to the upper or lower palate of the mouth. The dents and grooves in the mould are an exact impression of the gum and mouth.

Next, a plastic substance is put into the mould. When the mould hardens, it forms a plate that fits exactly over the gums. The teeth, usually made of plastic, are fixed to the plate, or **denture**. The base of the false teeth is held in place by a special adhesive. This keeps it in the mouth but allows the denture to be removed at night and for cleaning.

Plastics

Plastic is an artificial material that can be formed into almost any shape. It can be made as hard as iron or as soft as putty, and in any colour as well as clear.

Plastics are easy to shape because they are made up of long chains of **molecules** called **polymers**. Polymers are made of repeating patterns of smaller molecules, each one forming a link in the polymer chain. Some chains are rigid, like logs in a raft; others are tangled and flexible. The nature of polymer chains allows plastics to be shaped.

Usually, plastic materials are heated and then moulded into shape as they cool. Some, called **thermosets**, can only be heated once – they cannot be reused; others, called **thermoplastics**, can be reheated and recycled. Celluloid was the first plastic material to be widely used; items produced included combs, film and false teeth.

SYNTHETIC RESINS

Polymers are made by combining chemical compounds such as benzine and ammonia. Chemical reactions between the two cause polymerisation, which produces synthetic resin - the base plastic material. Resins can be made into pellets or powder, which is then heated and shaped.

Plastic objects come in all shapes, sizes and colours.

Inventor's words

denture
false teeth
impression
molecule
plastic • polymer
thermoplastic
thermoset

Make a set of false teeth

You will need

- air-hardening clay
- blunt knife • strong glue
- elastic • card
- paints and brush

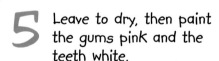

1 To make the lower set of teeth, model a large chunk of clay into a semi-circle. Push down the middle and build up the sides to form the palate (a horse-shoe shape).

2 With a blunt knife, cut into the gumline, marking 16 same-sized sections into the lower jaw.

3 Now mould the sections into teeth. Pinch the front sections to form 4 incisors, shape two eye teeth to a point and flatten, and round off the back sections to form molars. Repeat to make the top jaw.

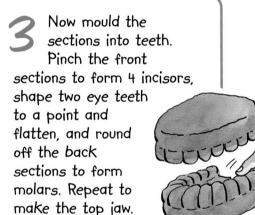

4 Glue one end of a piece of stretched elastic to the back of the top jaw and the other to the back of the bottom jaw, overlaying each with a piece of card and more glue to secure.

5 Leave to dry, then paint the gums pink and the teeth white.

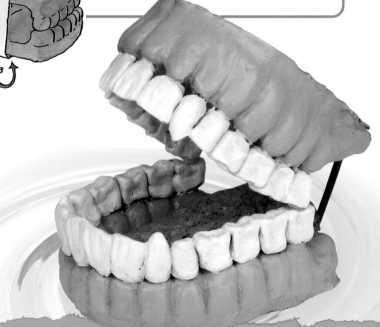

Clatter your teeth like castanets, and make them chatter!   7

How can I prevent disease?

Not so long ago, when people caught a disease, they became seriously ill. Diseases such as smallpox caused blindness or left people terribly scarred. Often, they died. Children were not considered to be safe from smallpox unless they had survived the illness.

Little was known about smallpox other than that it spread easily and that most people caught it, sooner or later. Survival rates were low and many people died. Doctors didn't know how to treat it. But they did know people could only get smallpox once.

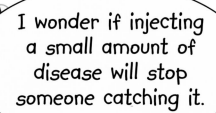

I wonder if injecting a small amount of disease will stop someone catching it.

People thought that if they took pus from a smallpox sore and infected themselves, they might get just a mild dose of smallpox and then be safe. But it was risky. However, the practice gave physician Edward Jenner an idea.

WHAT DID HE DO?

- Jenner knew that many country folk told an odd story. They said that dairymaids who had caught cowpox, a disease similar to smallpox, never caught the more serious disease.

- So, in 1796, Jenner tried an experiment. First he took pus from the hand of local dairymaid Sarah Nelmes, who had caught cowpox. He then made two cuts in the hand of James Phipps, a healthy eight-year old boy, and injected the fluid into them.

- Sure enough, James caught cowpox from the pus, or vaccine, that Jenner had injected into him. What would happen to James next?

Well, I waited 48 days before injecting young James with smallpox pus, just as I'd done with the cowpox. Then I waited again. James didn't catch smallpox. The original injection of cowpox had prevented it!

Within a few years of Jenner's experiment, vaccination became the accepted method of treating smallpox. In the twentieth century mass vaccination throughout the world eradicated the disease.

Germ attack!

A **vaccination** is a dose of medicine made from a **vaccine**. A vaccine contains the germs, which may be living or dead, that cause the disease. Vaccines may also contain the poisons produced by the germs. Vaccinations are given by mouth, by scratching the surface of the skin or by an injection.

The vaccine causes the body's **immune system**, or natural defenses, to attack the germs. The immune system not only gets rid of the tiny amount of the disease caused by the vaccination, but it also creates a permanent defence against future attacks from the same kind of germs.

Immunity

The immune system is the body's defence against illness. It is made up of a number of different parts, including white blood cells, which are made in bone marrow, lymph nodes and the spleen. Lymph nodes and the spleen produce lymphocytes, special white blood cells that fight against infections.

When harmful bacteria or viruses enter the body, they produce substances called antigens. The lymphocytes react to the presence of antigens and make antibodies, which attack and kill the invading bacteria or viruses. Some of the white blood cells, called phagocytes, go to the site of the infection and surround the invading bacteria, as if they were eating and destroying them. A vaccination gets the white blood cells up and running, so they can instantly protect the body from the bacteria or virus they need to attack.

VILE VIRUSES

A virus is a tiny germ. It is much smaller than bacteria and can only be seen through a powerful microscope. A virus can only survive in living tissue. Different viruses attack different kinds of cells in the body, causing diseases such as measles and 'flu.

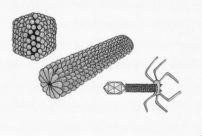

White blood cells help to protect the body from disease and infection.

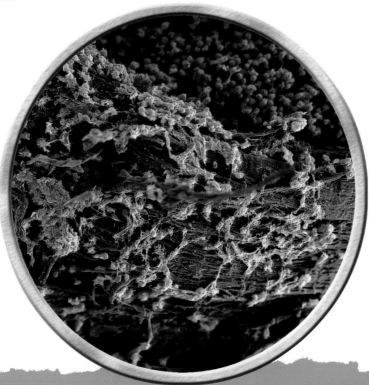

Inventor's words

antibody • antigen
bacteria
immune system
lymph node
lymphocyte
phagocyte
vaccination
vaccine • virus

Make a cell showcase

You will need

- A4 sheets of acetate
- acrylic paints and brush
- bubble wrap
- shoebox
- hole punch
- thin wire
- sticky tape

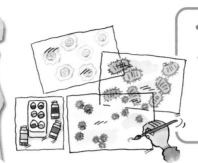

1 Paint cell-like shapes on to a sheet of acetate. Repeat on two more sheets, changing the cell-shapes and the colours used.

2 Glue bubble wrap on to the base of a shoebox and paint the inside walls white or pink, or another cell-like colour.

3 Make 3 holes at regular intervals down each corner edge of the box. With a hole punch, make holes in all 4 corners of your acetate plates.

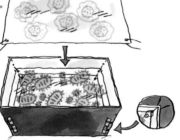

4 Take one of the acetates and thread a piece of wire through each hole, and then through each of the lowest holes in the corners of the box. Bend the wires to fix and secure with tape on the outside.

5 Repeat with the other acetates. Now paint and decorate the outside of your cell box.

Can I operate without hurting?

War, illness and accidents always cause pain and suffering. Sometimes, the injury is so bad that a limb needs to be cut off, or an internal organ repaired or removed. In the past, operations like these used to cause more shock and pain than the injury itself.

The first surgeons operated on a patient as best they could. There were few ways they could reduce the pain or shock of the operation.

One method was to knock patients out with a mallet. But that was not a good idea as the blow could kill them!

What can I give to my patients to numb their pain?

Another way of reducing the discomfort of an operation was to give patients a lot of alcohol to drink. They might pass out or get tipsy enough not to mind the sight of the saw or knife.

WHAT DID THEY DO?

- In 1800, Sir Humphrey Davy, a British chemist, suggested using an anaesthetic, a drug that kills feeling, in the body. He recommended the gas nitrous oxide.

- No one took much notice until 1844, when Horace Wells, an American dentist, used it on himself before having a tooth pulled out.

- Meanwhile, in 1842, Dr Crawford Long had a patient breathe ether, another anaesthetic substance, until he became unconscious.

- But the credit for using anaesthetic was given to William Morton, a dentist from Boston, in 1846.

Dentists were the first to use anaesthetics, but they were soon taken up by doctors, too.

Anaesthesia

An **anaesthetic** is a drug that causes a loss of sensation, or feeling, in the body. This loss of feeling is called **anaesthesia**. There are two kinds of anaesthetic: general anaesthetic and local anesthetic. A general anaesthetic causes loss of feeling in the entire body. It makes a patient unconscious and unable to feel any pain.

General anaesthetics can be swallowed, inhaled or injected. Local anaesthetics cause a loss of feeling in a specific area or part of the body. The patient stays conscious during the operation. Local anaesthetics are usually injected. In 1853, Queen Victoria was anaesthetised during the birth of her eighth child, Prince Leopold.

Painkillers

Anaesthetics are made from drugs that work on the body's nervous system. They stop certain nerves called sensory nerves from causing the feeling that we call pain. Sensory nerves carry pain signals to the brain to warn us of injury or illness.

When a general anaesthetic is injected or inhaled, it makes its way into the bloodstream of the patient's body very quickly. It then travels to the brain. There, it blocks, or cuts off, the electrical impulse messages that tell the sensory nerves to register things, including pain. With the messages blocked, the body feels nothing and recognises nothing. It is, in fact, unconscious. The patients act as if they were asleep.

It takes just 30–60 seconds for patients to become unconscious, and a few minutes to wake up, although they may feel drowsy for a while.

SAFETY FIRST

When people are under a general anaesthetic, they lose control of their reflexes and cannot move. At the same time, their heartbeat and breathing slow down. A trained anaesthetist must be present to monitor the patient's condition throughout an operation and help with the breathing.

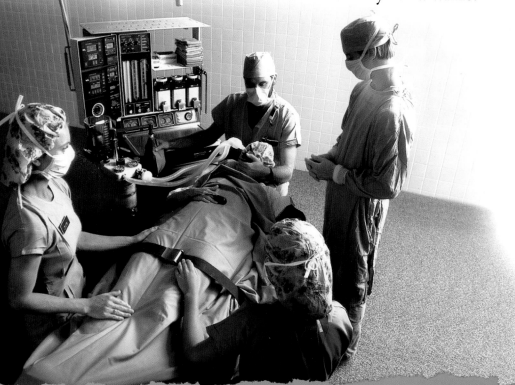
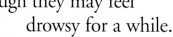

Modern anaesthetics make it possible for surgeons to carry out complex operations that can last many hours.

Inventor's words

anaesthesia
anaesthetic
sensory nerves

Make a funky stethoscope

You will need

3 plastic tubs:
1 medium, 2 small
• plastic tubing
(from shopping bag handles)
• wire • card
• double-sided tape
• cork coasters • glue
• paints and brush

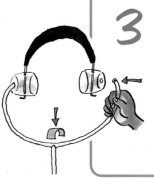

1 Make a hole in the top of the larger tub and push through a piece of plastic tubing.

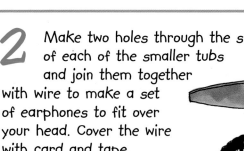

2 Make two holes through the side of each of the smaller tubs and join them together with wire to make a set of earphones to fit over your head. Cover the wire with card and tape.

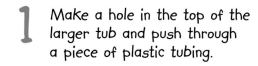

3 Make a hole in the base of each tub and join them together from below with a piece of plastic tubing. Cut a notch in the centre of it, and fit the first tub and tubing. Tape over the join to fix.

4 Cut 2 cork coasters into ear protectors and glue them on to the earphones.

5 Paint and decorate your stethoscope in bright colours.

Can you hear your stomach gurgle?

How can I prevent infection?

When soldiers are wounded in battle, the surgeons do everything they can to heal the injury. But often the soldier dies anyway, even if the wound is small. When ordinary people are injured, doctors also try their best, but it's almost impossible to treat infected wounds.

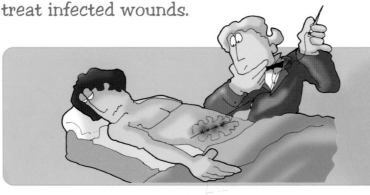

Joseph is a doctor. He does his best to heal his patients but many are dying from infected wounds. No matter how careful he is, wounds still get infected.

No one knows what causes the infections. With more operations being carried out using anaesthetics, infection is an added problem.

Can invisible microbes that carry disease be found and destroyed?

While Joseph practices medicine, a French chemist called Louis Pasteur writes a paper that says the air is filled with tiny, invisible microbes, or germs, that might be able to carry disease. This interests Joseph.

WHAT DID HE DO?

- Joseph Lister studied Pasteur's work on microbes. He concluded that pus in a wound is due to germs.

- He decided that during an operation everything, including the patient's wound, had to be kept as germ-free, or antiseptic, as possible.

- Ordinary washing wasn't good enough, though. Lister had to destroy the microbes. But how?

- Carbolic acid kills bacteria germs. Perhaps spraying the air with this antiseptic substance would do the trick. It worked, but it was still not enough to prevent infection.

> I'll have to do more than just spray the operating theatre. There are still germs on our hands and instruments. So I'll insist that my antiseptic is used on them. I'll also apply antiseptic to the dressing on my patient's wound.

After the introduction of antiseptics, the death rate from post-operative infection fell from 50 percent to 15 percent.

Germ buster

An **antiseptic** is a substance used to prevent infection in living things. It kills germs such as **bacteria** and prevents them from spreading. Antiseptics are applied to the skin and open wounds. The first successful antiseptic, using carbolic acid, was invented by Joseph Lister, a professor of surgery, in 1866.

Antiseptics must be strong enough to fight germs but mild enough not to irritate the sensitive tissue they are applied to. Each carries a germ-fighting chemical, such as alcohol, mercurials and salycimides. Surgeons scrub their hands with special antiseptics before operating. They also spray antiseptic on to serious wounds.

Bacteria

Bacteria are tiny living things. Each one is made up of just a single cell. Most bacteria are harmless, but some can cause diseases when they invade other organisms. They are so small, measuring as little as .001mm, that they cannot be seen without a microscope.

Bacteria reproduce by dividing into two. Each new cell is the same as the original. There are thousands of species of bacteria. They live almost anywhere and are even found inside animals, including humans. Most of these bacteria live in the **intestines** and help digestion. Useful bacteria also destroy other harmful organisms and produce some of the **vitamins** the body needs. Harmful bacteria cause diseases such as cholera, influenza and scarlet fever.

KILL OR CURE

Before the introductions of antiseptics, surgeons on the battlefield noticed that untreated wounds smelled of rotting flesh. They tried to cover up the stench with anti-sepsis, or anti-decay, substances such as brandy, tar and even turpentine. Some of these substances killed the germs - but they also killed the patients!

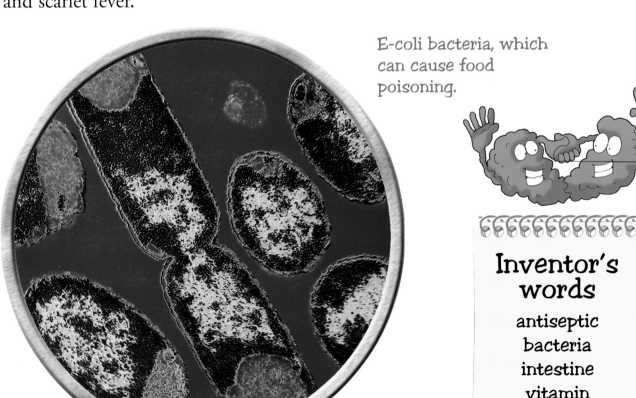

E-coli bacteria, which can cause food poisoning.

Inventor's words

antiseptic
bacteria
intestine
vitamin

Make your own lab critters

You will need

- scissors • acetate
- stapler and staples
- PVA glue
- air-drying clay or plasticine
- feathers, buttons, drawing pins
- pipe cleaners
- paints and brush

1 Cut circles from acetate. Next, cut out acetate strips and staple the ends together to make rings the same size as the circles.

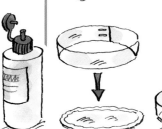

2 Glue the rings on to the circles to make petri dishes.

3 Make lab critters from clay or plasticine, and decorate them with feathers, buttons and drawing pins. Stick clay balls on to pipe cleaners for eyes.

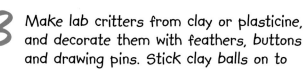

4 Paint your critters in vile colours once the clay is dry.

Now serve them up on their petri dishes! 19

How can I give drugs quickly?

Early doctors gave medicine by mouth, which takes a long time for the body to absorb. The time it took could make the difference between life and death. If medicine could reach the bloodstream more quickly, lives would be saved.

Many physicians knew that getting medicine into the bloodstream as quickly as possible was vital. One way was to spread a lotion directly on to a wound.

An even better way was to use a thorn to prick the skin, then put the medicine in through the tiny wound.

Taking medicine by mouth was safer, but it took too long, or the medicine didn't get to the right place. Francis Rynd thought a special needle could be used to inject medicine under the skin and into a vein.

What kind of needle can I use to inject life-saving drugs directly into a patient's bloodstream?

WHAT DID HE DO?

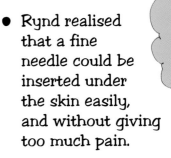

- Rynd realised that a fine needle could be inserted under the skin easily, and without giving too much pain.

- But somehow it had to get medicine into a vein as well. The answer was to make the needle hollow.

- Medicine could then be pumped through the needle and into the patient's vein.

- But what kind of pump could do the job? It certainly couldn't be a steam pump! It had to be something simple and small.

Yes! I'll attach a kind of plunger pump to a barrel. Then I'll connect the barrel to a hollow needle. When medicine is put into the barrel, the plunger will pump it out into the needle... and straight into the patient's vein.

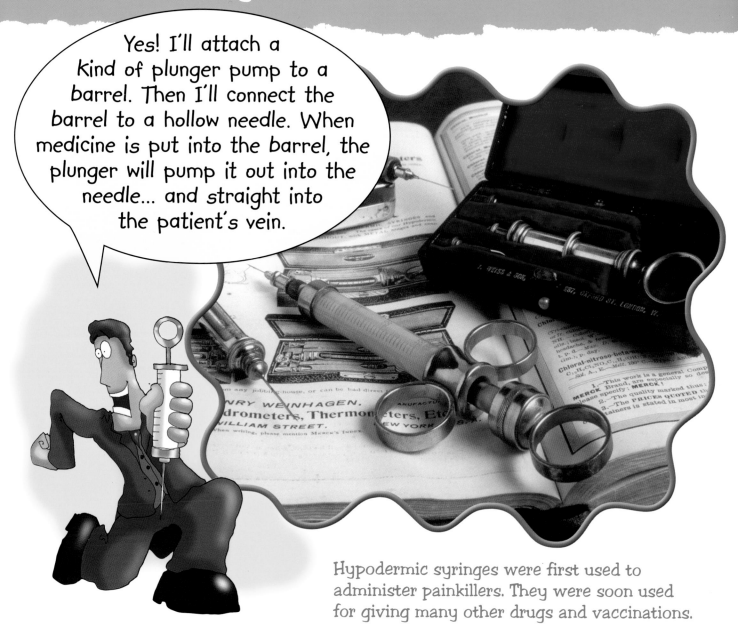

Hypodermic syringes were first used to administer painkillers. They were soon used for giving many other drugs and vaccinations.

Under the skin

A **hypodermic syringe** is a medical instrument that allows drugs to be given under the skin. It consists of a tube with a small piston or plunger inside that is attached to a sharp, hollow needle. The hypodermic syringe was invented in 1845 by Francis Rynd, an Irish physician.

A more practical metal syringe was invented in 1853 by French physician Charles Pravaz. The first syringes were made of metal and were used many times. Today's syringes are made of plastic. They are used just once and then thrown away. Syringes can also be used to remove blood from a patient.

Pumps

A **pump** is used for moving a liquid or a gas. Pumps are used in many different machines and other devices. Around 250 BC, the Greek inventor Ctesibius made a reciprocating pump, with a to-and-fro motion, for pumping water.

A reciprocating pump is a pump that uses the actions of a **piston** inside a **cylinder**, or tube, to pump water or gas. When the piston moves in one direction, it allows the liquid or gas to enter the cylinder. When it moves in the opposite direction, the piston pumps, or pushes, the water or gas out of the cylinder. In a hypodermic syringe, the cylinder is attached to a hollow needle that is open at the tip. The piston pumps the medicine through the needle and into the patient.

ROUND AND ROUND

Most modern pumps are operated by a rotating set of blades called an impeller. As the impeller turns, the blades trap the substance to be pumped and force it through the pump system..

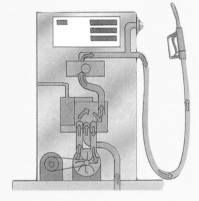

In some parts of the world, people still collect water from a pump.

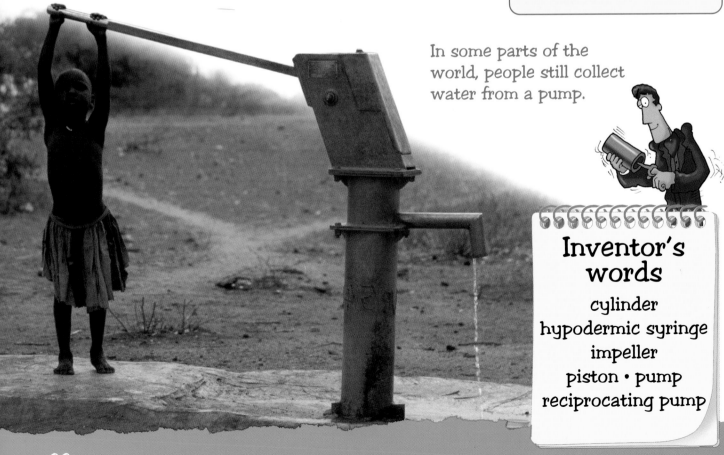

Inventor's words

cylinder
hypodermic syringe
impeller
piston • pump
reciprocating pump

Make a hypodermic syringe

You will need

- craft knife
- thin cardboard tube
- paints and brush
- cardboard
- foam board
- double-sided sticky tape
- strong glue
- white card
- plastic straw

1 Cut a long window down the length of the tube, as shown. Paint the inside red and seal one end with a card disc.

2 Cut 6 discs of foam board to fit inside the tube. Cover the edges of each one with double-sided tape or strong glue, and roll them up in a length of white card to form a cylinder.

3 Stick a piece of card to the end of the paper cylinder to make a plunger. Do the same at the end of the cardboard tube, but cut a hole in it so the plunger can slide in.

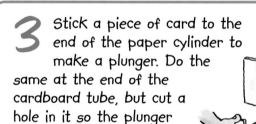

4 Glue a small piece of tube to the top of the plunger and fit a card disc at the end to cover the hole.

5 Make a small hole in the bottom of the outer tube and glue a plastic straw in place to make the needle. Decorate your giant syringe.

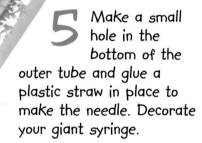

Pull out the plunger and take aim!

How can I stop food spoiling?

Even when food is easily obtained, it's not always easy to keep. Many foods such as milk become sour if they aren't used quickly. Sometimes, people are forced to eat food that is bad because there is no fresh food. Even wine can go off.

Wine-makers in France were worried. Their wine was bitter and no one knew what caused the problem. They wouldn't be able to sell unpleasant-tasting wine.

Louis, a brilliant young chemist working in Paris, thought he knew the answer. He studied tiny germs called bacteria.

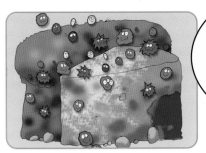

He knew that bacteria live almost everywhere. He even proved through his studies that living things can only come from other living things. He wondered whether the bacteria living in the wine were causing the problem.

There must be a way of controlling these beastly bacteria!

WHAT DID HE DO?

- Louis Pasteur spent a great deal of time examining bacteria. Other scientists had also studied them, but he believed bacteria caused changes in the substances in which they lived.

- He studied a process called fermentation, in which microbes such as yeast and bacteria cause a chemical breakdown in substances.

- Some fermentation can be helpful, when making bread, for example. But others can be harmful.

- Pasteur discovered that bacteria caused fermentation, which turns substances like milk sour. He also found a way to control them.

I'm sure it's the bacteria that's making the wine taste so foul. I'll control the bacteria by heating the wine to a high temperature. The heat will kill them off. Now I'll enjoy drinking fine wine.

Pasteurisation improves the safety of food and gives it a longer shelf life.

Controlling germs

Pasteurisation is a method of preserving food, or keeping it fresh. It is usually used for preserving liquids such as milk, wine and beer, but it is also used to preserve many other foods such as cheese and eggs. Food is harmed by certain kinds of **bacteria** that make people very ill.

These bacteria multiply in the food and cause it to go bad. Pasteurisation involves heating the food to a specific temperature for a short amount of time. For example, milk is heated to 72°C for about 15 seconds. The process kills any harmful bacteria and makes the milk safe to drink.

Bacteriology

Bacteriology is the study of bacteria, or the tiny living organisms we call germs. Louis Pasteur was the first person to show that living things can only come from other living things. Before him, scientists believed that bacteria-like organisms could come to life spontaneously, or without some kind of parent.

Pasteur also discovered that although bacteria lived almost everywhere, their spread could be controlled. This was important because, while most bacteria are harmless or even beneficial, some can cause dangerous diseases. In the early 1860s, Pasteur used his studies of bacteria to save the wine industry in France. He also proved that diseases are caused by a build-up of bacteria in the body. He experimented with animals in his laboratory and found that weakened amounts of the bacteria injected into them gave them **immunity**, or freedom, from the disease. His experiments showed how vaccinations work.

Scientists working in food laboratories make sure that the food we buy is safe to eat.

SILK SAVER

In the mid 1800s, the silk industry was in trouble. A disease called pebrine was killing the silkworms. Louis Pasteur found that bacteria were attacking the silkworms' eggs and that this was causing the disease. By using his heat method, Pasteur killed the bacteria and saved the silk industry.

Inventor's words

bacteria
bacteriology
pasteurisation
immunity
spontaneous

Make a crazy scientist's mask

You will need

- large balloon • strips of newspaper • PVA glue
- scissors • wool
- double-sided sticky tape
- toilet paper • card
- thin wire • acetate
- rubber bands
- paint and brush

1 Cover half a balloon with layers of newspaper soaked in a solution of half glue, half water. Leave to dry. Pop the balloon and cut out eyeholes.

2 Attach strips of wool to double-sided tape to make hair panels. Stagger the panels together to create a full head of hair and a beard.

3 Soak toilet paper in watered-down glue and sculpt eyebrows, eye bulges, nose and lips. Add card ears. Paint your mask.

4 Make specs out of thin wire and add acetate lenses. Make a hole on each side of the mask, thread rubber bands through and tie in place.

Put on your mask when performing experiments

How can radiation cure disease?

Sometimes the body produces cells that grow out of control and destroy other cells nearby. Early scientists and doctors didn't know what started the cells growing. And they certainly didn't know how to stop them. These cancer cells caused a lot of pain and suffering.

The diseases caused by cancer cells are frightening. In the 18th century, some doctors tried to cure their patients by draining off some of their blood.

This usually left the patient in a worse state than before. Then, in the 19th century, scientists began to understand the causes of cancer.

Surely we can find some way of stopping cancer cells from growing out of control.

They realised that cell growth was controlled by chemical instructors in the body. If these instructors are damaged, cancer cells can grow and multiply out of control. Eventually, they can destroy the body.

WHAT DID THEY DO?

- Scientists wanted to find a way of destroying the cancer cells without killing off the healthy cells around them.

- Operating on a patient was one way of removing the cells. But early operations without anaesthetic were as dangerous as the disease itself.

- Then scientists studying certain substances noticed they gave off energy in the form of radiation, or wave energy, which destroyed everything in their path.

- In 1889, in Paris, Marie and Pierre Curie discovered that a substance taken from uranium ore also gave off radiation. They called this material radium.

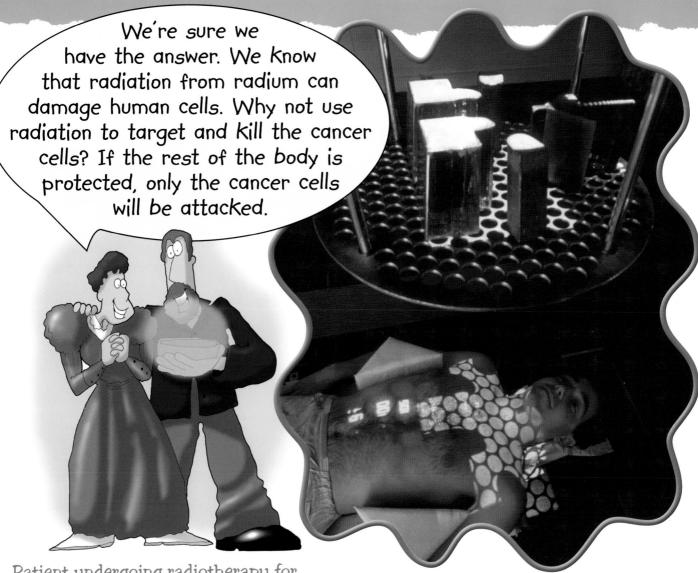

We're sure we have the answer. We know that radiation from radium can damage human cells. Why not use radiation to target and kill the cancer cells? If the rest of the body is protected, only the cancer cells will be attacked.

Patient undergoing radiotherapy for Hodgkinson's Disease, a type of cancer.

Treating cancer

Radiotherapy is a method of treating many kinds of cancer. The treatment uses invisible waves of energy, called **radiation**, to destroy cancer cells. Radiotherapy is often used after an operation to remove a **malignant** or active, growth of cells – cancer cells. The treatment kills any cancer cells left behind after the operation.

Radiotherapy attacks a **tumour**, or growth of cancer cells, with **radium**, x-rays or other radioactive substances such as cobalt. Modern radiotherapy uses two new devices, super-voltage x-rays and the cobalt bomb. Cobalt bomb radiotherapy can penetrate further into the body yet causes less damage to the skin and healthy cells.

Gene genius

Genes **are the control systems in the body that determine what cells do. They control how a cell multiplies or stops multiplying. They also instruct cells on how they can repair themselves when damaged.**

Genes are found in **chromosomes**. Every cell in our body has 46 chromosomes. Twenty-three come from the mother and 23 from the father. They are made from a chemical called deoxyribonucleic acid, or **DNA**. Every chromosome carries about 1000 genes that are strung together in a chain that looks like a twisted rope ladder. Our genes determine all of our physical characteristics. For instance, people who have genes for 'short person' in their chromosomes will be short. If the genes that govern cell growth and division are damaged, the cells can grow out of control. This uncontrolled growth creates cancer. Some cancers can be hereditary or caused by allowing harmful substances such as nicotine from cigarettes into the body.

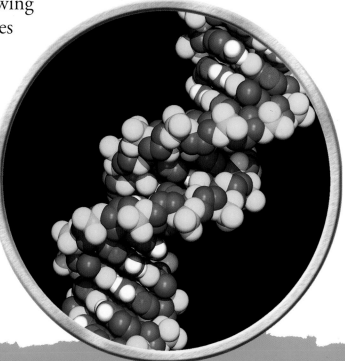

Model showing the structure of DNA, which consists of two twisted strands, known as a double helix.

DANGEROUS ENERGY

Radium is a silvery-white metallic element that is found mainly in uranium and thorium ores. Over time, uranium breaks down as it gives off radiation energy. This eventually changes it into a different substance called radium. Radium continues to be radioactive and so is very dangerous.

Inventor's words

chromosomes
DNA • genes
malignant
radiation
radiotherapy
radium • tumour
x-ray

Make an x-ray skeleton

You will need

- clay or plasticine
- paint and brush
- pipe cleaners
- tall cardboard box
- wire
- strong glue

1 Make a head, arms and lower legs out of clay or plasticine and paint them. Make sure the ends of the body parts are flat so they can be easily glued to the side of the box.

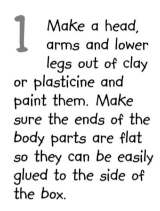

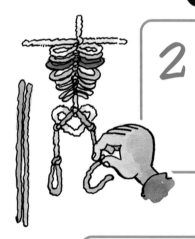

2 Use pipe cleaners to make a *skeleton* that will fit neatly into the box.

3 Attach the *skeleton* to the inside of the box with small pieces of wire and strong glue. Then glue on the head, arms and feet to the sides of the box.

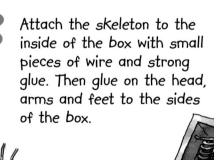

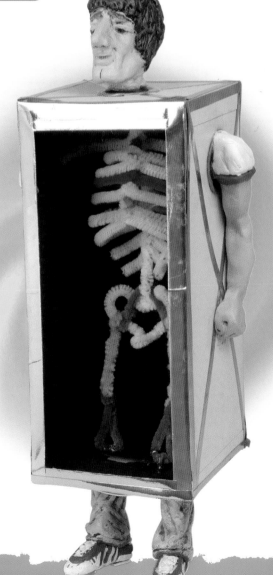

The human skeleton is made up of 206 bones!

How can I check a heartbeat?

Doctors can tell whether your heart is beating quickly or slowly by feeling your pulse. But this doesn't tell them anything about your blood pressure. Listening to the heart is useful, but something more is needed to help diagnose heart irregularities and diseases.

In 1628 William Harvey published his ideas showing that the heart works like a pump. But doctors still didn't know how to treat heart problems.

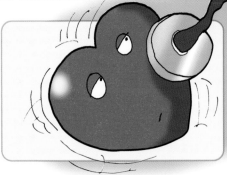

Rene Laennec, a Frenchman, invented the stethoscope in 1816. It gave doctors more information about what is going on in and around the heart.

Then in 1881, Siegfried von Basch invented the sphygmomanometer, a device that measured blood pressure without breaking the skin. But many diseases were still hard to diagnose.

We need to know what makes the heart beat to understand how it goes wrong.

WHAT DID HE DO?

- A Dutch scientist named Willem Einthoven studied the workings of the heart.

- He learned that minute electrical impulses, or currents, travel through the heart with each beat.

- He wanted to make a device that could measure the normal pattern of electric impulses in the heart. Then he would be able to tell if there were any abnormalities.

- In 1903, he invented a machine that recorded each variation, or change, in the electric impulses, even very tiny ones. Each impulse made a magnet in the machine move.

> I'll attach the machine to the patient, using small metal plates called electrodes. The electrodes will pick up the electric signals from the heart. If I attach a pointer to the magnet, it will write the pattern of each beat on a piece of paper.

Einthoven's electro-cardiograph, first known as a string galvanometer. The electrodes were jars filled with saline.

Wired up

An **electro-cardiograph** is a machine that records electrical activity in the heart. Doctors use it to diagnose heart disease. Wires run from the electro-cardiograph to **electrodes,** small metal plates that conduct electricity, which are fixed to the patient with a special jelly. The electrodes transmit the heart's electric signals to the device. Each beat of the heart produces an electric current, or signal.

The signal determines the kind of contraction, or beat, that is taking place. An electro-cardiograph picks up and records these currents as lines. It may be connected to a printer that prints out the lines called an ECG or **electro-cardiogram**, or it may be connected to a screen. Doctors look at the series of lines the device makes. They can tell which are normal and which indicate a problem.

Moving wires

When a wire carrying an electric current is in a magnetic field created by a permanent magnet, or close to it, the combined energy of the current and the magnetic field produces an electromagnetic force that is strong enough to move the wire.

Willem Einthoven used this concept when he invented his string galvanometer. He attached the wires from the electrodes to a fine wire coil, which was suspended in a magnetic field. When a current of electricity was fed along the wire and into the coil, the coil reacted with the magnetic field to produce an electromagnetic force, making the wire move. Einthoven then attached a lever to the wire that traced its movements.
The lever copied the wire's movements on to paper. Each heartbeat produced a series of wavy lines.

MEASURING CURRENT

A galvanometer is another machine that can also be used to measure current. As the amount of current determines the size of the electromagnetic force, the greater the current, the more a pointer connected to the coil will move. The needle moves along a scale marked in volts.

A doctor can recognise the different lines produced by high blood pressure or other diseases.

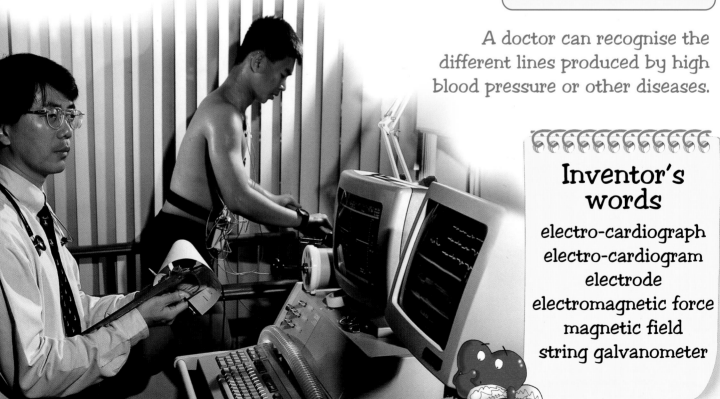

Inventor's words

electro-cardiograph
electro-cardiogram
electrode
electromagnetic force
magnetic field
string galvanometer

Make a heartbeat graph

You will need

- nails
- hammer
- wooden board
- coloured string
- PVA glue
- paints and brush

1 Ask a grown-up to help you knock in nails at roughly 1cm intervals around the rim of the board.

2 Once all the nails are in place, wind brightly-coloured string (you can paint it first) around them to make vertical lines.

3 Next weave the string horizontally through the vertical lines to form a grid.

4 Wrap different coloured string around the grid strands to make the zigzag shape of a heart beat.

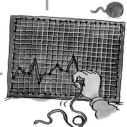

5 Make a frame for the string picture to cover up the nails, and glue in place with PVA. Decorate the frame.

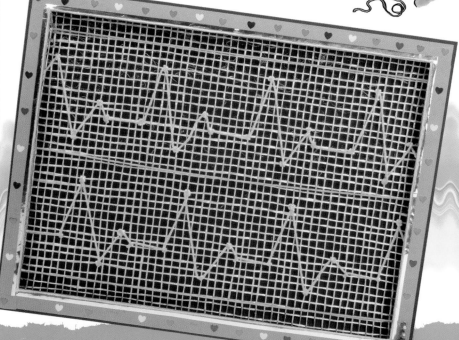

Can I keep a heart beating?

Sooner or later, everyone's heart wears out, but some give out quicker than others, because of disease or stress. Often, the heart is just unable keep up its regular beat. That means that blood can't be pumped properly around the body, causing illness or death.

People are living longer. Many more illnesses can be treated. But heart diseases are still a major problem. Some people may have weak hearts for hereditary reasons, or because they have a poor diet, or because they smoke.

During a heart attack, the heart may beat too slowly or too quickly. This can be fatal. A US scientist began to look at ways of regulating a person's heartbeat.

What can I use to make the heart beat in a regular rhythm?

WHAT DID HE DO?

- Modern medical equipment is getting better and better because of microchip technology. Smaller, more powerful machines can be made.

- At the same time, scientists are learning more about the heart and how it works.

- Scientists know that special cells send electric impulses, or nerve signals, through the heart, making it contract. When it contracts, or beats, it pumps blood through the body.

- If electrical impulses make the heart beat, perhaps a tiny machine could create the impulses for patients when their own system breaks down.

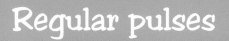

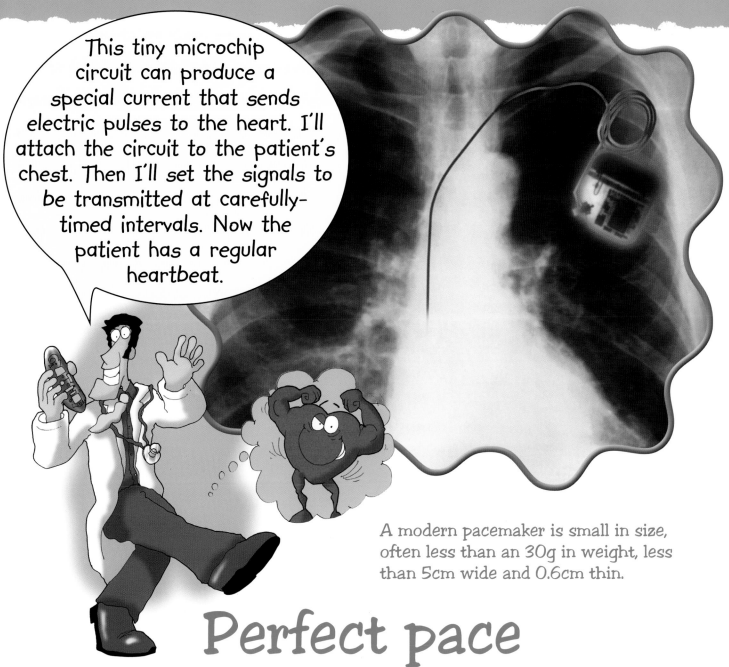

> This tiny microchip circuit can produce a special current that sends electric pulses to the heart. I'll attach the circuit to the patient's chest. Then I'll set the signals to be transmitted at carefully-timed intervals. Now the patient has a regular heartbeat.

A modern pacemaker is small in size, often less than an 30g in weight, less than 5cm wide and 0.6cm thin.

Perfect pace

A **pacemaker** is an electrical device powered by a small battery. It was invented in the late 1950s by Wilson Greatbatch, and is used by people with certain heart diseases that prevent the heart from beating regularly. The problem is called heart block, because the natural impulses that cause the heart to beat are blocked from doing their job.

The pacemaker is implanted inside the patient's chest and fixed against the heart. It sends out electrical impulses that cause the heart to **contract** at regular intervals. These impulses are created by a tiny **micro-processor**, or silicon chip, powered by a battery. Special pacemaker batteries have a life span of 10–12 years.

AC current

An **alternating current**, or AC current, is an electric current that behaves in a special way. The current grows stronger, then weaker and then changes direction. This happens many times each second.

Some microprocessors, called **oscillators**, convert direct current signals into alternating current signals. To oscillate means to vibrate steadily backwards and forwards. An alternating current oscillates, and a device that causes the current is called an oscillator. Oscillators can be used as **amplifiers**, like those used in music systems to boost sound. They can also be used for timing the signals that control computers in automatic machinery. A pacemaker is a type of oscillator. The alternating current produces carefully timed pulses that stimulate the heart to beat regularly.

ELECTRIC MISTAKE

In any kind of electric current, the electrons always move from the negative pole to the positive pole. But scientists describe the direction of the current as flowing from positive to negative. This is the result of a mistake made by scientists in the 1800s, who thought that electrons moved in that direction.

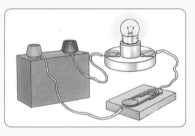

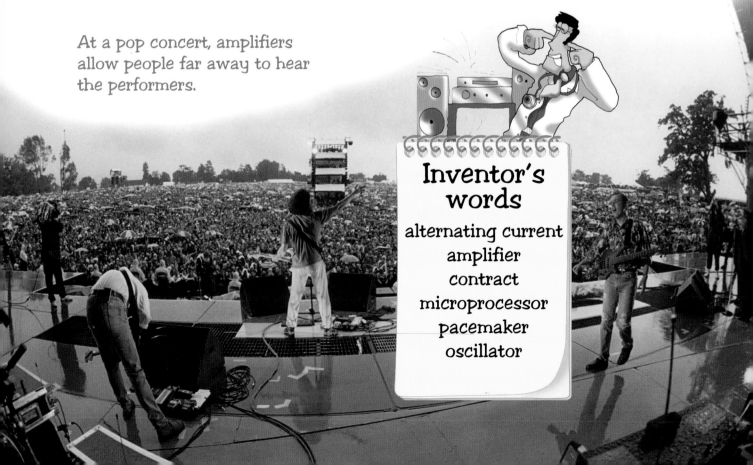

At a pop concert, amplifiers allow people far away to hear the performers.

Inventor's words

alternating current
amplifier
contract
microprocessor
pacemaker
oscillator

Make a keepsake box

You will need

- scissors or craft knife
- plastic bottle
- square cardboard box
- cardboard
- toilet paper
- PVA glue • acetate
- pieces of wire, screws, washers, nuts and bolts
- metallic paints and brush

1 Cut off the bottom of a plastic bottle and make a round hole in the top of the box for it to fit into. Snip around the rim of the bottle to make fold-out tabs and glue in place.

2 Make two cardboard dividers to divide the bottle end into 4 'keepsake zones'. Line with toilet paper soaked in PVA glue.

3 When dry, paint sthe inside and then fill up the compartments with nuts and bolts or keepsakes. Glue a sheet of acetate on top for a window.

4 Mould a 3D heart shape around the hole with toilet paper and PVA. Let it dry, then paint bright pink.

5 Decorate your heart box with tubing and more metallic bits and pieces such as wires, screws, nuts and bolts. Decorate with metallic paints.

Can you see inside a person's brain?

The brain is a very delicate organ. When something goes wrong with it, there is little anyone can do. Operating on it is dangerous, especially if you can't be sure what is wrong in the first place. If only it were possible to see inside the brain without an operation.

When something goes wrong with the brain all sorts of problems can arise. The brain sends out and receives hundreds of messages every second. It controls every activity in the body, from moving muscles to breathing. But it is made of very soft tissue, so it is protected by the hard bones of the skull.

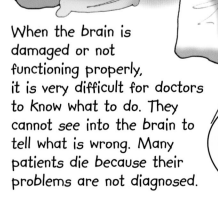

When the brain is damaged or not functioning properly, it is very difficult for doctors to know what to do. They cannot see into the brain to tell what is wrong. Many patients die because their problems are not diagnosed.

Is there a way to 'see' into the brain without operating?

WHAT DID THEY DO?

- In 1895 Wilhelm Rontgen, a German physicist, discovered x-rays. Within months they were used to view broken bones.

- A year later, Thomas Edison improved the fluoroscope so it could be used to view x-ray images.

- In 1913 William Coolidge devised a way to make an even more effective x-ray tube.

- With the development of computers and digital imaging, special detectors are used to measure x-rays that pass through the body. They send information to a computer that converts the data into an image that can be seen on a screen.

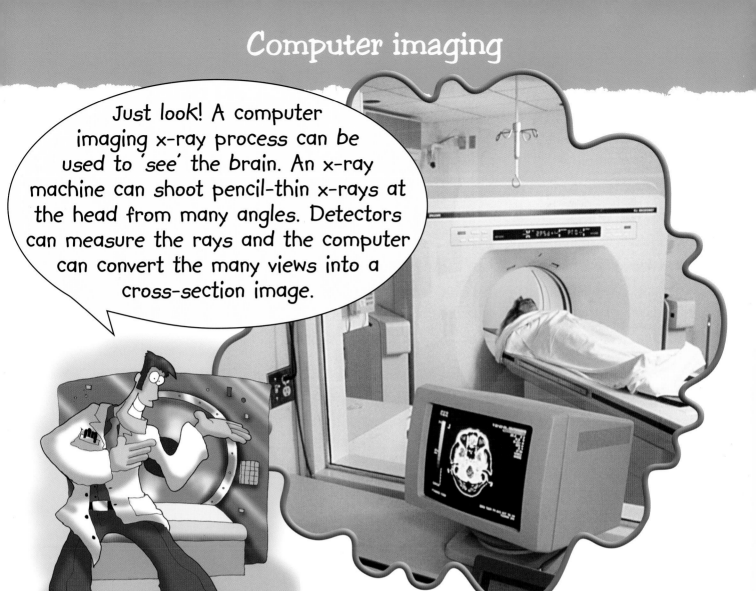

Just look! A computer imaging x-ray process can *be* used to 'see' the brain. An x-ray machine can shoot pencil-thin x-rays at the head from many angles. Detectors can measure the rays and the computer can convert the many views into a cross-section image.

The CAT, or computerised axial tomographic, scanner, allows doctors to see deep inside the body without the need for surgery.

Picturing the brain

Invented by Bernard Gordon in 1975, the **CAT scanner** is a machine used for taking pictures of the inside of the body, including the brain. It is made up of an x-ray machine and a series of detectors. The x-ray machine directs a number of very thin x-rays from different directions through a part of a patient's body. The rays then hit the detectors.

These detectors measure the intensity, or strength, of the rays and feed this information into a computer. The computer makes a cross-section picture of the part of the body that has been x-rayed. A CAT scan of the brain can tell doctors if there is an injury to it or if a patient is suffering from a tumour or some other kind of disease.

Super rays

The electromagnetic spectrum is a chart that lists the different kinds of radiation scientists call electromagnetic radiation. Electromagnetic radiation is a form of energy made up of both electrical and magnetic energies. It moves as electromagnetic waves, which are sometimes called rays. They move at 299,793km per second.

We can see some electromagnetic waves as the colours of light. This is called the visible spectrum. But most are invisible. Radio waves are at the top end of the spectrum, which means they have the longest wavelength, or distance between the peaks of each wave. We can hear radio waves but not see them. At the bottom end of the spectrum are gamma rays and x-rays. They have the shortest wavelength. They can also be very dangerous. **Gamma rays** are given off by atoms during **nuclear fission**. They can cause radiation poisoning, as can x-rays. That is why x-rays must be used with great care by radiologists who operate CAT scanners and similar machines.

GAMMA RAYS

Gamma rays have very high energy and are emitted from the nuclei of some radioactive atoms. Gamma rays can penetrate even better than x-rays so they are used in medicine to treat cancer. They are also used in the food business to kill micro-organisms.

A special lead apron protects patients from harmful rays.

Inventor's words

CAT scanner
electromagnetic radiation
electromagnetic spectrum
gamma rays
nuclear fission

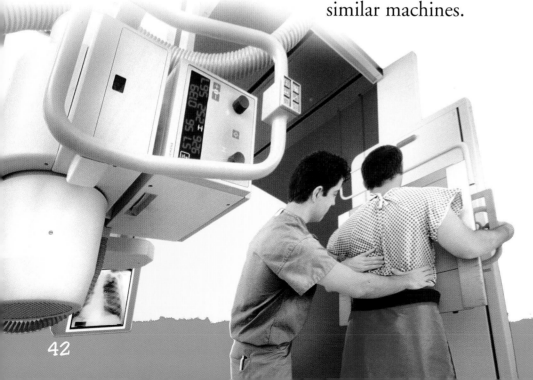

Make a decorative brain scan

You will need

- cardboard
- pencil • string
- strong glue
- tissue paper soaked in PVA (optional)
- paints and brush

1 Draw the silhouette of a head on a large oblong piece of cardboard.

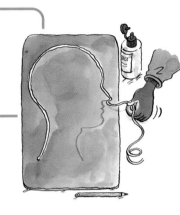

2 Glue along your pencil line and stick the string to it, following the outline of the head.

3 Draw in the detail inside the cross-section head – brain, eyeballs, teeth and spine. Again, glue over your pencil lines, then stick the string along the top.

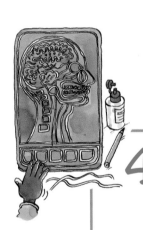

4 Design an information panel at the foot of your brain scan, as shown.

5 Line the background with tissue paper soaked in PVA if you want to raise it up for extra effect. Paint and decorate.

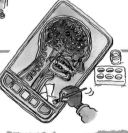

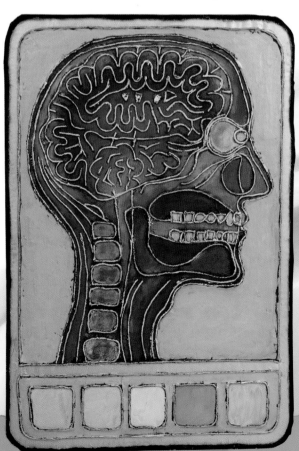

Glossary and index

Electromagnetic spectrum Chart that lists all the different kinds of electromagnetic radiation, arranged in order of frequency or wavelength. p.42

False teeth Artificial teeth that can be used in place of natural teeth. p.5, 6

Gamma ray Type of electromagnetic radiation. It has a short wavelength and high energy. p.42

Gene Control systems in the body that determine what cells do. They determine how a cell multiplies or stops multiplying, and instruct cells on how they can repair themselves when damaged. p.30

Hypodermic syringe Medical instrument that allows drugs to be given under the skin. It is made up of a tube with a small piston or plunger inside, which is attached to a sharp, hollow needle. p.21

Immune system Body's defence against illness. It includes white blood cells, bone marrow, lymph nodes and the spleen. p.9, 10

Immunity State in which the body is protected from viruses and bacteria. Vaccination can create immunity to some diseases. p.26

Impeller Rotating set of blades that operate most modern pumps. p.22

Impression Likeness of something. p.5

Intestine Long, coiled tube in the abdomen, through which food passes during digestion. p.18

Lymph node Part of the immune system. They are small lumps that produce some of the body's white blood cells and antibodies. p.10

Lymphocyte Special white blood cells that fight against infections. p.10

Magnetic field Field of magnetic force created by a permanent magnet. The field arcs between the north and south poles of the magnet. p.34

Malignant Description of a disease that may become worse, such as a tumour or cancer. p.29

Microprocessor Small part of a computer made up of integrated circuits. It controls programs and data. p.37, 38

Molecule Small particle containing two or more atoms that are joined together. A molecule of water has two atoms of hydrogen and one atom of oxygen. p.6

Nuclear fission Occurs when the nucleus of an atom is split, releasing huge amounts of energy. p.42

Oscillator Microprocessor that converts direct current signals into alternating current signals. p.38

Pacemaker Device that artificially controls the heartbeat. Wires from the pacemaker are connected to the heart. p.37, 38

Pasteurisation Method of preserving, or keeping fresh, food by heating it for a short amount of time. p.25

45

Phagocyte Part of the immune system. Phagocytes are white blood cells that go to the site of an infection. They surround invading bacteria and destroy them.　p.10

Piston Tube-like device that fits snugly into a cylinder and moves backwards and forwards. Pistons are used in internal combustion engines and pumps.　p.22

Plastic Solid substance made of artificially-made polymers.　p.5

Polymer Solid material composed of large molecules that are joined together in a chemical process to make a chain.　p.5

Pump Machine used for moving a liquid or a gas.　p.22

Radiation Movement of electromagnetic waves and photons, creating invisible waves of energy.　p.29, 30

Radiotherapy Method of treating many kinds of cancer, using radiation to destroy cancer cells.　p.29

Radium Radioactive element. It is a metal found in ores such as pitchblende.　p.29, 30

Reciprocating pump Acting in a to-and-fro motion.　p.22

Sensory nerve Nerve that sends messages to the brain about the senses. For example, sensory nerves in the skin send messages about touch.　p.14

Spontaneous Reaction carried out quickly, without conscious thought.　p.26

String galvanator Instrument for measuring small electric currents such as those produced by the heart.　p.34

Thermoplastic Plastic that can be melted down and used again.　p.6

Thermoset Plastic that cannot be melted down and used again.　p.6

Tumour Swelling in the body that may be a malignant growth such as cancer, which needs to be removed.　p.29

Vaccination Dose of medicine made from a vaccine. It is made from the germs, living or dead, that cause the disease.　p.9, 10

Vaccine Medicine for a disease made from the germs that cause it.　p.9

Virus Tiny germ that can only survive in living tissue. Viruses infect cells causing diseases such as measles and 'flu.　p.10

Vitamin Chemical substance found in the foods we eat. We need vitamins to keep healthy.　p.18

X-ray Type of electromagnetic wave with a short wavelength. X-rays have great energy and can travel through materials such as skin and flesh. They can be used to help treat disease. Also the photographs made by an x-ray machine.

p.29, 41, 42

Tools and Materials

Almost all of the materials in this book can be found around the house or bought at your local art or craft shop. If you cannot find the exact item, try and replace it with something similar.

Most of the models will stick fast with PVA glue or even wallpaper paste. However, some materials need a stronger glue, so take care when using these as they may damage your clothes and even your skin. Ask an adult to help you.

Always cover furniture with newspaper or a large cloth, and protect your clothes by wearing a work apron.

User Care

Take special care when handling sharp tools such as scissors, pointed gadgets, pieces of wire or craft knives. Ask an adult to help you when you need to use them.